You Were Made for This World

Celebrated Indigenous Voices
Speak to Young People

For our grandfather Elmer Sinclair, and all the residential school Survivors.

For our kids, Julian, Cole, Dakota and Madeleine, and all the children
who will carry this inheritance and build a better future.
— STEPHANIE AND SARA

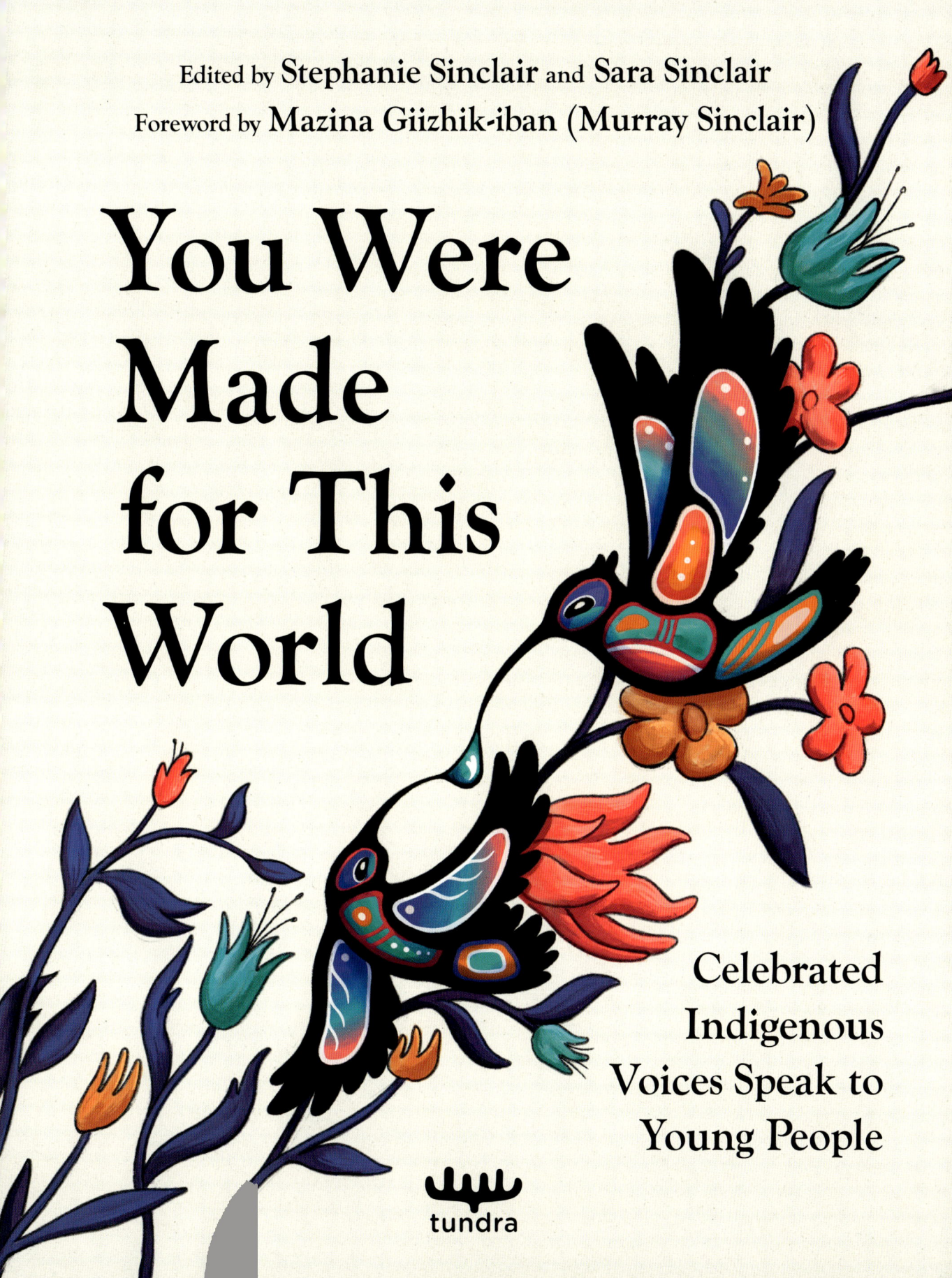

Edited by **Stephanie Sinclair** and **Sara Sinclair**
Foreword by **Mazina Giizhik-iban (Murray Sinclair)**

You Were Made for This World

Celebrated Indigenous Voices Speak to Young People

tundra

INTRODUCTION
How This Book Came to Be
by Stephanie and Sara Sinclair 11

FOREWORD
An Ugly Duckling
by Mazina Giizhik-iban (Murray Sinclair) 17

LETTERS 25

CONTRIBUTORS 108

NOTE ABOUT THE COVER ART 118

CREDITS 119

WATER

katherena vermette 25
Art by George Littlechild

Tanya Tagaq 29
Art by Jason Sikoak

Autumn Peltier
(Red Moon Woman) 31
Art by Luke Swinson

Jennifer Grenz 33
Art by Chief Lady Bird

Zoe Todd 37
Art by Ailah Carpenter

TOBACCO

Warren Cariou 43
Art by Leah Marie Dorion

Cherie Dimaline 47
Art by Alanah Astehtsi' Otsistóhkwaʔ (Morningstar) Jewell

Deidre Havrelock 51
Art by Denesee Paul

CEDAR

Cindy Blackstock 57
Art by Karlene Harvey

David A. Robertson 61
Art by Bryce Many Fingers / Singer

Pamela Palmater 65
Art by Alan Syliboy

Tasha Spillett 69
Art by Kaya Joan

Cynthia Leitich Smith 73
Art by Michael Nicoll Yahgulanaas

SWEETGRASS

Monique Gray Smith 79
Art by Daphne Boyer

Jesse Wente 83
Art by Christi Belcourt

Ethan Bear 87
Art by Maya McKibbin

Norma Dunning 91
Art by Ella Nathanael Alkiewicz

SAGE

Wab Kinew 97
Art by Mangeshig Pawis-Steckley

Brittany Luby 101
Art by Corrie Hill

Jessica Johns 105
Art by Jessie Boulard

INTRODUCTION
How This Book Came to Be

WHEN WE WERE SIXTEEN AND FOURTEEN YEARS OLD, we rode the train to a Sinclair family reunion. Our paternal grandpa Elmer's extended family was gathering on the grassy banks of Manitoba's Red River for a party. The day of the reunion was beautiful, the sky a perfect prairie blue, and in a rare moment of intimacy with Grandpa, we visited the graves of our ancestors, ending at the towering grave of Chief Peguis.

We began that trip in Toronto, where we grew up with our younger sister, Minoway. Our father, Douglas, is Nehiyaw-Anishinaabe (Peguis Nation). Our mother, Joanie, immigrated to Montréal from the UK with her family at the age of five.

When we were young children, our mom's mom, "Bubby" to us, moved from Montréal to our home in Toronto. Bubby was a German-Jewish refugee whose incredible imagination was our constant companion. She spoke often about the importance of a happy childhood — she told us how memories of her early years had helped her to survive the later, frightening ones in Nazi Germany. Bubby's own grandmother, her beloved oma, refused to flee Germany, a decision that ultimately cost her her life. Our home was filled with Bubby's watercolor paintings, paintings that evoked the German fairy tales her oma had read to her as a child. Their shared inner world was a part of our environment, there for us to engage with whenever we wished.

Our dad's parents, Granny Phylis and Grandpa Elmer, visited every year from Winnipeg. We grew up a little more removed from their stories.

Along with 150,000 First Nation, Métis and Inuit children in Canada, our grandfather Elmer had survived an Indian residential school. From age seven to ten, he lived at the Catholic Fort Alexander residential school. Fort Alexander was one of approximately 130 such schools in Canada. In the United States, there were 357, where they were known as Indian boarding schools. The schools removed Native children from their families, and the kids were not allowed to speak their own Indigenous languages and their cultural practices were forbidden. Children often suffered physical and sexual abuse at the hands of the authority figures tasked with managing their education.

Bubby was open about the therapy she had undergone to recover from the traumas of the war and its aftermath. We knew her history well. She had left Germany in January of 1939 and arrived in London, age twenty-one, alone and impoverished. The war raged on, and just a few years later, the intense aerial bombardment over London forced our bubby to separate from her two young children, our auntie Sheila and uncle Michael, who were among 650,000 children evacuated from London to the English seaside for protection.

Over the decades, Bubby recovered her ability to share her earlier memories with our mom and with us. However, our dad left home when he was a teenager, and the strains and silences in his family hadn't healed in the same way. An important reason for this difference is that our bubby found strength in telling her story. To feel healed, a person needs to feel heard. The Holocaust's horrors were acknowledged. Stories about it were taught in school and shared in movies and on television. And when Bubby spoke, she connected her listeners to this bigger history. Unfortunately, in Grandpa Elmer's lifetime, Survivors of Indian residential schools didn't receive the same support when they shared their experiences. Only very recently has the history of these schools been included in Canada's education for young people.

Our grandpa Elmer didn't talk to us about his experience directly, but we've now seen the description he shared with our uncle Warren: "The three years in that school [were] the saddest days of my life. The nuns and the priests were about the most cruel people God ever created. I could never imagine how people who confess, or said they were servants of God, could be so cruel to children. I have never forgotten that." One consequence of his years spent at the school was shame. Our grandfather became a decorated soldier in the Canadian army; his courage was celebrated many times over. But he did not tell his own seven sons that they were Indigenous. When our father learned, at age eight, that he was, he remembers feeling surprised and then feeling his own shame. In childhood games of Cowboys and Indians, he had played the cowboy, the good guy, not the Indian, who was always the villain.

As we grew up, it became clearer that Bubby seemed to heal through telling her story, and that so many stories untold by Indian residential school Survivors meant so much history unhealed and unknown.

In different ways, we both grew interested in connecting the past to the present; in our professional lives, we both work to amplify stories like our grandfather's. Steph does this as a publisher and Sara as an oral historian. We know from our own family's experience that when traumatic events occur in cultures and are left undiscussed, it's not just the stories about the traumas that don't get passed down. The transfer of other cultural knowledge is disrupted too. Our grandfather, for decades, didn't share stories about his own family or his young life, because he was taught to be ashamed of being an "Indian." And then, unintentionally, he passed down that shame instead of stories.

Part of the learning, begun by our father and continued by us, is to more deeply understand that many Indigenous people alive today have grown up at some distance from their ancestors' stories. This is a direct and intentional consequence of colonization, of which the Indian residential schools were an important weapon. For many, being Indigenous is a journey toward reclamation and continuance of language, knowledge and nationhood.

And now we each have two children of our own, Grandpa Elmer's great-grandchildren. We want them to learn more of their stories. We want them to understand all this history, to know both its burden and beauty.

This book is an offering along this journey. Structured as a medicine bundle, with each letter representing a traditional medicine — water, tobacco, cedar, sweetgrass or sage — this anthology is an entry point to conversations we want to have with our children. We hope these words and images might also move you toward conversations about Indigenous history, strength and life, conversations many of us struggle to begin.

In the final weeks of work on this book, our beloved Murray Sinclair passed away. We want to especially acknowledge the role that Murray Sinclair had in starting so many of these conversations on a national level and with each of us. We send forever thanks to Murray, for teaching compassion, for listening to all of our stories, for believing us and for believing in us. Thank you for helping awaken so many of us to who we are.

We wonder, did this country deserve you?

We know you would want us to say yes.

All knowledge is produced through relationships. And we are immensely grateful for the beautiful words and images that this book's collaborations have created. Each piece offers a space to continue to learn and change with grace, just as Murray did, and just as he led.

To our project's contributors: This book's range, its power and its joy are testament to each of you and your unique gifts. It is an honor and a privilege to share these pages with you — to experience the beauty and insight of your art and words. Thank you for your truthful and hopeful offerings.

To our readers: Welcome! We are so happy you are here to honor who we are, the land we are on and the medicine we all need to find our way forward.

— STEPHANIE AND SARA SINCLAIR

FOREWORD
An Ugly Duckling

AS A LITTLE BOY, THE FIRST TIME I HEARD the story of the Ugly Duckling, I was touched by it. Something about it spoke to me. The story of a bird being raised in a family of ducks, who was told he was a duck, who was even loved as much as the other ducklings by the Mother Duck, but who never felt right and eventually finds redemption as a swan, was uplifting. I identified with him. He believed he was a duckling, and he tried hard to be a duckling, but all the other ducklings made fun of him. They kept telling him he was not as beautiful as the other ducklings and never would be as good as any of them. They called him the Ugly Duckling. He came to see himself as less than the others. No matter how hard he tried, he knew that he would never be accepted by them, and he would never be as beautiful as they were. He simply did not look like them. He felt shame.

I identified with the little Ugly Duckling because of the shame I felt growing up poor. Because of our poverty, we were not only unable to fulfill our wishes, we also had difficulty meeting our basic needs. When you grow up without money, you can't buy the same clothes as others, you can't go to the same events or participate in the same activities as your friends. Even the lunches you take to school can be a source of shame. You make up lies to explain such failures and you learn how to manage those lies. Shame can make you feel shy and awkward in almost all social situations.

Yet when I look back at my youth, I have to admit that after a certain point, I was anything but shy. I was outgoing, brash, a jokester and not afraid to ask a question or express a thought. I challenged people. Yet I knew much of that was learned behavior — a facade to cover up a deeper lack of confidence.

When I graduated law school and started practicing law, I continued to feel like a fraud, but on a grander scale. I felt I didn't deserve to belong to that profession, a feeling written about by Pauline Rose Clance in her book *The Impostor Phenomenon: Overcoming the Fear That Haunts Your Success*. Added to this was a feeling that I should not be where I was, that I was participating in an ongoing process of injustice. I was torn over my sense of what law was, and what justice and fairness meant. I was caught between the perception of law I had learned at school, and the perception of law carried by Elders. They were different — yet the Elders' perception was as deeply felt and absolutely as valid as anything taught at law school. It was an understanding of law that appealed to the core of me, but that I could not reconcile with what I was being asked, indeed required, to do as a professional lawyer.

I was also torn over other personal decisions I had made. I felt tremendous stress over having brought children into this world without having the capacity to be a proper father to them. I felt enormous guilt over the fact that I was never going to be able to give them a sense of their history, and their future, as Anishinaabe. I felt that all I had been taught to accept as being important was no longer relevant and amounted to immense self-deception. I didn't lose my sense of direction, I lost faith in it. I really did feel like a failure.

I came close to quitting the law career I had chosen but was persuaded by an Elder named Angus Merrick — to whom I will always be grateful — to think instead about those things I had never been taught, things that were central to being Anishinaabe. I saw the wisdom of what he told me, and I set out on a journey of discovering Anishinaabe identity, not just for myself, but also for my children. I am in year forty-five of that journey.

The story of the Ugly Duckling has risen in importance for me because what it teaches us still has relevance. Like so many other Aboriginal people of my generation, I had been raised, like the Ugly Duckling, to believe I was something I was not, and I really believed what I had been told. I strove hard to be like every other student. In fact, I was smarter and stronger and faster than most of them and enjoyed greater success. Yet I knew that most Canadians did not — and never would — accept me as one of their own. They saw me as something less than them. I could see it in the history books we studied in school and in the images on TV and in the movies. As Willie Nelson said, in the title to his song, "My Heroes Have Always Been Cowboys," and mine had always been too. Yet our cowboy heroes despised Indians, and I suspected that if we ever met, they wouldn't like me. I could hear society's disrespect for me and my ancestors in the stories that were spoken and the ones that were not, in the public comments that were made and the jokes that were told. I could see it in the eyes of strangers when I passed them on the sidewalks. I felt it in the poverty we lived in and in the lack of opportunity, which was a challenge for me to overcome but was never an issue for so many others.

Many with whom I came into contact tried to be fair, and I felt their love and acceptance and support, but the general treatment of Aboriginal people by mainstream society told me that because I was Anishinaabe, the prevalent stereotypes would be mine to bear. I would always be an Ugly Duckling.

Yet in the story of the Ugly Duckling, hope and pride prevail. The Ugly Duckling grows into a beautiful swan and discovers that he was always a swan and never a duck. More importantly, he learns how beautiful he really is. A bird can look ugly as a duck, not because he's ugly but because he's not, in fact, a duck — he's a swan with his own beauty. It is significant that the Ugly Duckling does not discover his beauty from the society of ducks. He learns that from other swans.

I feel the same way. I have learned, and continue to learn, what it means to be Anishinaabe. I have learned in the process that, just as the little Ugly Duckling was always a beautiful swan, I have always been a beautiful human being, belonging to a group of other beautiful human beings with a proud and distinct history and existence. I have learned that, like the duckling/swan, I can still hang out with ducks, but I don't have to try to be a duck — I can be a swan. The swan does not diminish the duck. They can all still fly together. Diversity is natural and not something that needs to be overcome. It need not threaten the unity of humanity. It was not the swan who needed to change, it was the ducks who were called upon to recognize the wrongness of their behavior. Accepting and coping with our diversity as humans calls for accommodation, trust and respect.

That's, in fact, what reconciliation is all about.

That's why I continue to love this story.

— MAZINA GIIZHIK-IBAN (MURRAY SINCLAIR)

Water is the first medicine, because none of the others can grow without it. In Anishinaabe teachings, Nibi (water) is the blood of Aki (Earth), a sacred energy that is part of us, flowing within and between us.

Words by katherena vermette
Art by George Littlechild

Tawnshi, you,

I want this letter to be a pack of wishes. I want to send these words out into the universe, out to Creator or whoever is in charge, so that if these wishes are not true now, then they will be one day soon:

Young cousin, I wish you LOVE, so much love you can't even stand it, so much you push it away and say, "Gimme some space, love. I get it!" I want you to have love like that, the kind that's all yours, every day.

I wish you PEACE, the kind of peace that comes from knowing that you and your world are safe and calm. The kind of peace that gets under your skin and keeps you warm all night. I wish you peace like that.

I want you to have HAPPINESS, not just the Christmas morning kind you get from getting all the good stuff, but the real happiness that comes from doing and being and thinking exactly what you want, the true happiness that comes from feeling what you want to (which is usually happiness). I mean, people usually pick to feel happy, but if you'd rather feel annoyed or angry, that's okay too. As long as you don't hurt anybody, you can feel whatever you'd like, right? They are your feelings. But I hope you choose happiness, at least some of the time.

I hope you KNOW YOU ARE AMAZING. You are. We are so lucky to have you in this world, and you can do literally anything you want to. I mean it. Find your dream and go after it. You can make it work. You're flipping amazing, after all. It will take work, and you will probably give up once or twice (or many, many times), but get back up and keep going. Life is for living, Amazing One. Keep going and you'll get somewheres, for certains.

Okay, if you don't believe anything else, believe this: without a doubt, you are a SUPERHERO! Your ancestors have been through so much to get you here, and the fact that you are alive, that we all are, is proof we are superheroes. Those who came before us are mighty and powerful and still here with you. You are NEVER ALONE, young cousin; you have an army of ancestors behind you, all rooting and cheering for you. You also have me, and all us aunties and uncles and auncles and cousins who only want the best for you. We love you, young cousin. Never forget that. You have LOVE and an army and you are a SUPERHERO.

Maarsii for being here on this planet with me.

k.

Words by Tanya Tagaq
Art by Jason Sikoak

Dearest precious,

Run on the grass
Throw rocks
Throw snowballs
Cheer at the sun
And protect your heart

Take that jump on your bike
Grab at the clouds
and eat them like cotton candy
Stare into the moon
And protect your heart

Watch ants cross a stream
making a bridge with their bodies
Clutching and cooperating
Working and marching
We protect our hearts

Share your smile
open and full of laughter
Receive the rain
Splash in the puddles
And protect your heart

Your heart is so precious
Life is magical
Your laughter lights up the sky
Your tears are the rivers
Your breath is the wind
Love yourself
And protect your heart

Words by Autumn Peltier (Red Moon Woman)
Art by Luke Swinson

In a country like Canada that is so rich in resources and culture, our water and our planet shouldn't have to suffer. We need to find ways to preserve our waters for future generations, as this has been a prophecy of our people. The prophecy states that one day, an ounce of water will cost as much as an ounce of gold, and one day, we will be fighting over clean water.

When you wake up each day, do you enjoy being able to drink fresh water from the tap? My people are the original stewards and peoples of this land and have suffered many years without access to clean drinking water. My people have suffered enough and for far too long. Children should be able to drink water from their taps across Canada and the world.

I was a child when I began to worry about what kind of future I would have.

Mother Earth takes care of us without ever asking anything in return. We need to give back and help the water and the planet. They need our voices.

Use your voice like I have chosen to use mine.

Words by Jennifer Grenz
Art by Chief Lady Bird

Dear Frog,

Oh, the stories you have to tell us.
Stories from two worlds.
The water and the land.
You must have so many stories,
knowing twice as many relations as me.
Is this why you have so much to share
in the dark nights when you sing me to sleep?
I was drawn to you from the time I was small,
a curiosity that has never waned.
Searching for you in the trees and the tall grass.
In the ponds, and streams, and ditches.
What secrets can you tell me?
I watched you emerge from your egg,
swimming with your brothers and sisters.
Were you sad or scared when you grew legs
and lost your tail?
Or had you been waiting for it with excitement?
In anticipation of what came next?
I watched you leave the only world you knew.
You hopped out of one
and into another without hesitation.

You hopped so quickly
it was difficult to follow you with my eyes.
How did you already know how to do that?
How do you do it?
This living between two worlds.
I hear you in the trees sometimes
and I am amazed at how you can climb.
I catch a glimpse of you back at the pond you emerged from,
still swimming with the grace of a fish.
My, how you have changed
from that wiggling tadpole.
You are a window into a world
I cannot physically visit myself.
You bring me stories I would otherwise not know
as you move effortlessly from the water world
to my own upon the land.
Are you sharing my stories
with someone in the water I do not know?
One day the water calls you back
so your next generation can begin.
You need the water and land.
Sometimes we forget that we do too.

Thank you for your songs.
They are a reminder of our relations
in worlds we do not know.
A reminder of our shared reliance
upon the worlds you bridge.
A reminder of our responsibilities to care for them.
Thank you, Frog,
for my perpetual curiosity
to seek you and the wisdom you carry.
My life is better because of you.
I wonder if the fish think so too?

Words by Zoe Todd
Art by Ailah Carpenter

There are places that will hold you even when you have moved far away from them.

When I feel lost, scared, alone or unsure of what to do, I close my eyes and conjure up the banks of the North Saskatchewan River/kisiskâciwani-sîpiy (in nêhiyawêwin). I imagine the sandbanks rising up from the river's fast-flowing prairie waters. I picture the aspen trees leafing out in bright green at the start of spring. I visualize the critters around me — the whitefish, the sturgeon, the crayfish, the saskatoon bushes, horsetails, willows, dragonflies and butterflies. I breathe in the smell of silt and damp and new leaves and potential.

For a moment, I pretend I have stepped out of the busy world of emails, social media and work, and pause with the river in my mind. And I feel at peace.

Water, whether it is an ocean, a lake, a waterfall, a river or a creek — it has the power to carry us through generations and centuries to speak to and with the people who came a long time before us.

Sand and water hold entire worlds together.

I am grateful that no matter where I am, I can conjure up the waterways, the sands, the hills, the forests, the prairies and the vast oceans that many ancestors before me moved through to help me find my way through my life today.

As I pull myself away from the North Saskatchewan River in my mind and head back into the busyness of my day, I will leave you with one final thought: What places do you carry with you?

Tobacco is used as an offering. "Always through tobacco," as the saying goes. When we make an offering of tobacco, we communicate our thoughts and feelings through it.

Words by Warren Cariou
Art by Leah Marie Dorion

Letter to Ni-câpân Eleonore,

Ni-câpân, my great-grandmother: all I have of you is a few stories, some documents, a photograph. Is that enough for me to say I know you?

One thing I do know is that you were born in a place called Forget. Your parents were traveling far from home, following the buffalo, and so you entered this world on the open prairie, in a district where none of your family had ever lived. Except that's not quite true, because in a way, your descendants were all born into a different kind of forgetting, the one that came when the government tried to erase us. It happened so quickly, and you witnessed it all.

You were two years old when Canada began. By the time you'd grown up, the buffalo were gone, the Métis nation had been attacked twice by the Canadian army, and our people were uprooted from their land, called traitors, forced to eke out their living on the edge of roads. Many were killed or disappeared.

How did you survive that time? How did you raise your children in the aftermath? I want to understand, but there are so few stories, so few records to tell me.

Still, today is a time of remembering, Ni-câpân, a time for bringing back as much as we can. In our family, what we remember most about you is your determination, your fierceness and the fact that you were a midwife, bringing generations of children into this land.

In the one photo I have of you, you're sitting outside in winter with Great-Grandpa John, neither of you wearing coats or gloves. Your hands, folded in your lap, are even larger than his, and there is something in the casual way you hold them that reveals great strength.

I imagine your grip — powerful enough to do a man's work on the land, yet gentle enough to coax a reluctant newborn into an unwelcoming world. What prayers did you speak to those children? What comforts did you give to the mothers? How did you share your strength with them?

You've shared it with us, through all these years and even through the time of great forgetting. A future was born into your strong hands and those of your Métis midwife sisters. I am so grateful to be a part of it.

— Ki-câpan, Warren

Words by Cherie Dimaline
Art by Alanah Astehtsi̱' Otsistóhkwaʔ (Morningstar) Jewell

Dear fifteen-year-old Cherie,

Here's the thing, and maybe it's actually two things that are connected. First, you have everything you need to be a storyteller. Second, you will have to search for what you need to be a storyteller.

You have been given a great advantage, being raised by storytellers. So, the first step is to recognize your grandmother and your great aunties for who (or what) they are, not just card sharks who like to gossip, but card sharks who tell great stories, who are in fact magical in their ability to weave a tale and protect memory. You were raised inside of the world's best story school — Aunt Flora's kitchen, back home on the Bay.

The way that you get shy in class because the answers you want to give are never simple? That's because you want to answer the questions with story. Because the way that you have been taught has always been through the rhythm of story. The problem is that you also see stories as personal — intimate hieroglyphics expressing the shape and weight of lived experience. What you have is the rhythm of story. What you need to find are the ways to make story public.

You read more than anyone else you've ever known. This makes you feel both connected and completely alone. This ability to find real connection in other people's stories is what you have. The ability to draw people close to your own story — like a small, hot fire on a cold night — that is what you will have to find.

The way to find your voice and your power as a storyteller? This will involve both a recognition of what you have and a commitment to continue the search for what you don't. It will be many years before you meet your first real live author, but that is the moment when you'll realize that the author is both the person with the great privilege of having story and the person who will never stop searching for that which they don't have. That the author is both the map and the wanderer trying to find their way forward. And since there is nothing you love more than being (safely) lost for a short period of time, somewhere magical like the forest behind your house or in your imagination while sitting in the tree house, you will become an author. Remember this on the days where the loneliness and uncertainty feel biggest. A lost person with a map is only an adventurer, after all.

Words by Deidre Havrelock
Art by Denesee Paul

Dear Dede,

I know when you lie down to sleep, you feel terrified, like darkness has come alive to swallow you whole, the house expanding, creaking and groaning in its presence. When I close my eyes, I hear your sweet voice whispering out prayers to Creator. I hear you when you say, "Please, God, are you there? Please, God, can you help me?"

I need you to know that I am reaching out to you, stretching my hand back in time, grasping your small hand in mine. Can you feel my hand holding yours? I am here in the darkness with you. You are not alone.

Dear child,
You are not alone.
I am praying with you.

Dear Dede,
I know you sense a bad spirit slipping across your
room through the pale moonlight. I hear your heart
beating a fretful rhythm against your chest — Pa-PUM!
Pa-PUM! Pa-PUM!

I need you to know that I also feel that bad spirit, and
I am not afraid. I am here in the darkness with you,
strong and fearless, filled with perfect love.

Dear child,
Do not be afraid.
There is no room for bad spirits in the light of love.

Dear Dede,
I know your thoughts, discouraging and gloomy. I hear
you tell yourself that life will never change and that
you will always be scared. Too petrified to move.
Too frightened to speak.

I need you to listen to my voice. I am here in the
darkness with you, calling you blessed. You are every
good thing. And you shine with Creator's glory.

Dear child,
Listen to my words
for they will not stop
until darkness has lost its power
and we fall asleep embraced in Creator's peace.

— Deidre (Dede)

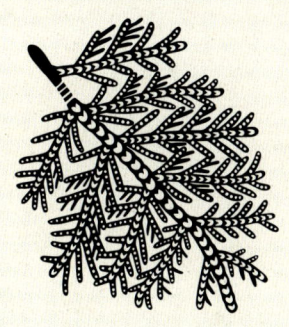

Cedar is used to purify the home and also offers protection.

Words by Cindy Blackstock
Art by Karlene Harvey

Dear First Nations children and young people,

You are the generation that our ancestors dreamt of, that residential school and Sixties Scoop Survivors sacrificed and fought for, and to whom we owe what the late Elder Elmer Courchene called "loving justice." You have a right to grow up safely with your family, get a good education, be healthy and feel proud of who you are.

For too long, governments treated you like you did not matter, like you should be thankful for getting less. Then Jordan River Anderson was born. He showed us that "being patient" and accepting "good enough" fuels discrimination. His death required that we act boldly, wisely and honorably to achieve loving justice. We know we can get to a place where all First Nations children and young people can live healthy, dignified and happy lives because we see how far we have already come.

As your grandparents, parents, aunties and uncles, our promise is that we will continue to fight for you. We will honor the sacrifices and collective efforts of Elders, residential school and Sixties Scoop Survivors, the children who were lost to both systems, and current generations of First Nations children, youth and families. We will be honest, base our work on the best ideas and evidence, say when we are wrong, take nothing that is yours and keep you at the center when we make hard decisions.

Unfortunately, some of the injustices will remain after we are gone. That is why we will also work to educate all people so they can stand with you to achieve justice. This is the duty we owe to the ancestors and to the residential school and Sixties Scoop Survivors who passed down the best of themselves, so that we have this chance to make the world better for you.

We will do our best for you, because we love you.

Words by David A. Robertson
Art by Bryce Many Fingers / Singer

You're no older than eight, and you ask your auntie Joan if you're ugly. Kids make fun of your brown skin at the pool. You don't understand why, and ugliness seems the only logical reason. Auntie Joan says, "Your skin is beautiful," but you start to hide anyway. You wander the house at night, in the darkness, searching for a different answer to your question. It's hard to find things in the dark, so you just make yourself tired.

When you learn that you're Indigenous, it doesn't help. If anything, it makes things worse. You trade wandering for wondering. You are confused. How can you be Indigenous when you are nothing like what you've learned about Indigenous people from movies, comic books and friends? Never mind the jokes that people tell at school. The ones that you laugh at so kids won't make fun of you anymore.

In high school, you tease a girl for asking if you're half Black because your head is shaved and your skin gets so dark in the summer. When she asks about your cultural background, you won't tell her. She calls you shallow, but really, you are lost. You sit with a friend on the crumbling stone wall of an old fort and call yourself a half-breed.

Over time, you learn about who you are through stories, and eventually, you start writing your own stories. You write stories so kids don't feel the same way that you did. Sure, there are times when you walk into a room and wonder why people want to listen to anything you have to say or read any story you have to tell, but healing doesn't happen overnight.

You find the best mentor in your father. You ask him why he never taught you how to be Cree. You lament how much better you would have been for it, and he tells you that you are exactly who you're supposed to be. That he can't teach you how to be something you already are. That a few ignorant kids calling you ugly doesn't mean that you're not beautiful. That part of the journey is figuring it out for yourself. That all those struggles make you stronger.

And because of that, because you will struggle, because you are strong, all I want you to know is that it gets better. So just hang on. One day, you'll find your way out of the dark and you won't be tired anymore.

Words by Pamela Palmater
Art by Alan Syliboy

Nuji'j, my grandchild, I am kukumij. I am your grandmother. Did you know that I have loved you since long before you were even born? It's true.

I have daydreamed about you my whole life. Ever since I was a young girl, I knew I wanted to have grandchildren. Now that I am grown up and have had children of my own, I wonder if you will one day look like ngwisk, my sons.

Will you have big, round, brown eyes like my eldest son, Mitchell? Or will you have sweet, droopy, blue eyes like my baby son, Jeremy?

Will you sing like a jipji'j, a bird? Or will you help kujj, father, fish on the sipuk, the river? Or maybe you will help kiju, mother, cook dinner?

I think about you so often these days that I think you must be on your way to me. Do you know how I know this to be true? Nkamlamun, my heart, feels like it is getting bigger and bigger and bigger!

Did you know that as a kukumij, a grandmother, I have a very important role? E'e, yes!

I get to love you, care for you and teach you the ways of L'nuk, the ways of the people — the Mi'kmaq. I get to help raise you along with your parents, aunties and uncles. You will always know unconditional love and support.

We will go out on the land and share our ancestors' teachings about how to protect nm'tginen, our homeland. We are the protectors of Mi'kma'ki, which means we have a responsibility to share these lands with all living things, including the fish, birds, bears and trees.

I will share with you all the special a'tukwaqann, stories, passed down from our ancestors, so you can enjoy the ways of our people with love and pride. Then, you will pass on our language, culture and traditions to your grandchildren someday. In this way, kniskamijinaqik, our ancestors, live forever.

Nuji'j, my grandchild, mi'walul, I am grateful for you, and I will always be here for you, now and forever.

Ma'munigsalul, I love you very, very, very much!

Words by Tasha Spillett
Art by Kaya Joan

To the ones who will inherit this world and especially to the ones who feel on the outside: Belonging is something that took me most of my life to catch in my hands and root in my heart. As an Afro-Indigenous person with mixed European ancestry, I spent a lot of time feeling like I didn't quite belong. I even changed my physical appearance to try to fit in. The sizzle of a hot flat iron on my damp and tender scalp was a price that I willingly paid to look just a little more like others in my community. But no matter how I tried, I somehow still felt like an outsider to the Indigenous community I was raised in and the Black community I was raised without.

As a young person, I understood my identity as a mosaic of fragmented pieces — pieces of different shades and shapes: some edges smoothed with love and joy, others left jagged by pain and displacement.

As I got older, I started to see myself not as scattered fragments but as a complete person, formed by all those I came from.

The world can be a messy place, making it difficult to see the good mixed up with all the bad. Hope can be hard to find, but it's there if you look.

On a warm and sunny day in September when my daughter was a baby, I noticed the neighborhood kids gathering outside the school across the street. I held my baby up to the window so she could watch the big kids laugh and play. She giggled with joy as a small group of those children waved at her. I found hope in her smiling eyes and in this simple gesture of welcome from across the street: Hope that this new generation will not carry the same pain and cruelty as those that came before. Hope that children will learn to see and celebrate the dignity in one another, and remember to care for one another.

With love,
a neighborhood mom

Words by Cynthia Leitich Smith
Art by Michael Nicoll Yahgulanaas

H esci, Dear One,

You may know me from my books as Cynthia Leitich Smith, a Muscogee author who writes stories about young Native heroes like you. But you can call me Auntie Cyn.

When I was your age, the supposedly Native characters in storybooks didn't make any sense. They seemed like wild things or magical beings or Elders who talked like Yoda from *Star Wars*.

Don't get me wrong. I love Yoda and *Star Wars* too, but I didn't figure out that people like us belonged in the world of books until after I was a grown-up. That's because I didn't see Indigenous characters in stories who laughed and loved and struggled and persevered. Characters who rang true.

I wanted better for you. We Indigenous people are the original storytellers on this continent, and we have a long, strong literary tradition too. What's more, these First Nations authors are speaking first and foremost to you.

Indigenous voices are vital and valued, and that includes your voice too.

Your rising voice is welcome and needed, powerful and appreciated.

You are a natural-born storyteller. It's a legacy of your ancestors, your culture, your family. Your voice is an echo and blessing of all the Native voices that came before. And it's uniquely yours.

Share it thoughtfully and with a loving heart — through story, through song, through prayer and, yes, on the page like me, if that calls to you. I can hardly wait for what you have to say!

Your Forever Fan,
Auntie Cyn

Sweetgrass is usually braided, dried and burned. It is used to cleanse and bring positivity.

Words by Monique Gray Smith
Art by Daphne Boyer

Câpân

I am Noel, ki-câpân.

Sadie, Jaxson and Brianna, you are ni-câpân.

I am here when you look back.
You are there when I look forward.

I am the sunset.
You are the sunrise.

I am winter.
You are spring.

I am leaves beneath your feet.
You are flowers blooming.

I am amongst the stars.
You are the stars.

I share messages in your dreams.
You are the dreams of many.

I am the one whose life was not gentle.
You are the ones I sacrificed for.

I am a vet from the Korean War.
You are the freedom we fought for.

My three children were taken from me and raised by
non-Indigenous families.

Your families are raising you with love, care and
connection to culture.

Cree and Michif flowed off my tongue with ease.
You will be on a language reclamation
and learning journey your entire lives.

For much of my life, I waited for change.
You are the change.

Ki-câpân endured the darkness
so Ni-câpân can be the light.

Words by Jesse Wente
Art by Christi Belcourt

Dear Future Relations,

Today, I see a flower growing in a crack in the sidewalk.

It's orange and yellow and green.

It shouldn't be there, but it is.

Someone tried to cover it up and bury it, but instead it pushed through the crack to see the sun, and now the sun can see it, in return.

Instead of staying hidden, it has grown.

As I watch the flower, other people pass. Many don't seem to notice the flower. Maybe they are too busy, or maybe they can't see it, or maybe they don't think it is beautiful.

Some even step on the flower. A few petals press into the rough cement.

But the flower doesn't break. It doesn't go back
into the crack in the sidewalk.

The flower lies there for a while, on its side.
It looks sad.

But then the rain comes. Drops fall on the flower
and roll into the crack like tears.

The flower slowly gets up. Its head lifts toward the
rain clouds, refreshed for its next visit with the sun.

Soon, someone else joins me in watching the
flower. And then another person, and then
another, and then another. Soon, it seems like
everyone is watching that flower in the crack,
that impossible flower that grew, even when its
roots were buried under cement.

And, with everyone watching, the sun returns from behind the clouds. And the flower blooms even bigger. And the people begin to think that maybe it is the cement that doesn't belong.

And so we tear up that cement, so that more flowers can visit the sun. So that, in time, more flowers will grow and return the sidewalk to what it had been before.

All because of that one flower.

I see you.

That flower growing in a crack in the sidewalk.

I see you.

Love,
Uncle

Words by Ethan Bear
Art by Maya McKibbin

Experience as much as you can of the world. Try not to feel alone or be afraid. As big as the world sometimes seems, it's what you do with your mind that will help you travel on your journey. That's something I've learned over the years. With hard work and dedication, with sacrifice and love, I've made a path for myself in sport. Every day, I put one foot forward and take steps to improve myself as a person, so I can learn and grow. It doesn't get easier or harder. That's the way I approach each day. I can't control what will happen tomorrow, but I can control my attitude and my work ethic. That's what I wish I could have taught my younger self growing up and what I want to share with you today.

I learned my courage from my mom, my family, my wife. My mom believed in doing what's right for everybody, not just yourself. That's something I've brought with me to sport — the value of being a good teammate and being a good sport to your opponents. When you improve yourself and lift others up, you gain a sense of confidence and belonging.

My first step forward involved moving away from home. It was probably one of the hardest experiences of my life, leaving the reserve. I had a different accent. I looked different. I talked different. I was only fourteen years old and adjusting to a harder school, being behind in my education and trying to catch up. I learned the value of persistence, honesty and stepping out of your comfort zones. That's how you learn.

I was always scared to be social and wasn't very vocal. I thought I would be quiet and observe others until I felt I could properly communicate, until I found my place in the world. But you learn to communicate by being around people. Honestly, it's an uncomfortable thing sometimes, to have a conversation with someone who has different interests. But it can also be exciting to learn about why other people like certain things, what drives them, what's important to them. Everyone does different things, and not everyone has to like what you like. But in order to grow in your job or develop your passion, you have to talk to people, ask questions, and you have to ask for help.

My support for others is what has made me a good teammate. In a team game, you can't win alone. You have to make sure your teammates want to win as well. You want to make sure they are happy. When they are happy and comfortable, they compete hard. That's what makes a good team. So, for myself, I work hard, and I get along with everybody by being respectful and nice.

That's the way I was raised. I was one of the best on my reserve. Yet, we would lose to teams that I knew we could beat until I learned to include my teammates more and teach them what they needed to do to help me. From that, I learned the importance of teamwork.

I want you — all of you kids — to love yourselves and not be afraid of the world. Because as I was growing up, that's how I felt, a little scared, no matter how much family support I had. When you are trying new things and trying to win, it can get hard. But life is too short to dwell on the negative, on what could be or should be. It's about what you can do to help yourself grow and how you can help others be what they want to be — that's what's most important.

Words by Norma Dunning
Art by Ella Nathanael Alkiewicz

L etter to Joel:

Joel, I am so grateful for your breath. When my palm cradled your newborn head, I grew greedy for more of you. You peered deeply into my eyes and etched my voice inside of your soul. You allowed me to enter your heart. You filled a chasm that had been inside of me for twenty years. You are the firstborn of my first son.

Newborn babies look like the Old Ones. Wrinkles. Crooked fingers. Foreheads marked with worry lines. Creator blessed me by seeing you at birth so I will recognize you again decades from now, in the land from beyond. Your ancestors and I will never leave you. I am always here, beside you. I will hold you up in this life and the next. You are never alone.

Always be proud of who and what you are. Don't let the sneers of others twist your shape. Don't let their skin color affect yours. Don't let their mean words nest inside of you. You are not the Other. Our ancestors brought us here and to one another. Please remember one word. It is an easy one. Ma'na — thank you. Always be thankful, Joel.

Be thankful for the unseen and unexpected. Say ma'na to soft summer breezes and to cold polar winds. Give thanks to the moon and the sun and the stars that dance us from one day into the next. Say ma'na to the trees and know that they hear you. Say ma'na to the rocks along soggy shorelines. They have weathered more than you or me. Give thanks to the early dawn and try to guess what her golden fingers will touch next.

I am your anaanatsiaq. Your life makes my life new again. Ma'na, Joel.

Sage is used to prepare people for ceremonies and teachings, for releasing what is troubling the mind and for removing negative energy.

Words by Wab Kinew
Art by Mangeshig Pawis-Steckley

To be Anishinaabe,
pronounced:
ah-nish-in-NAW-bay

To be Anishinaabe means a lot of things
that you can't always put into words.

To be Anishinaabe means waking up,
saying good morning to Mom and Dad
and eating with the rest of the family.

It means rushing to school
where the big kids are,
and the teachers have so much to say that your mind races.

And then, at the end of the day,
speaking to each other the Anishinaabe way.
Miigwech — thank you!
Wiisinidaa — let's eat!
Kiizhawenimin — I love you!

To be Anishinaabe means
collecting dolls and stuffies,
and playing make-believe.

It means playing with cars and trucks,
bulldozers, cranes
and even everyone's favorite — excavators!

To be Anishinaabe means
running around with your friends,
and playing hockey and soccer and basketball,
the sports that you love.

It also means doing all the activities
your parents sign you up for,
and trying your best
even when you're tired of being so very busy.

It means using phones and tablets
and apps and computers,
and listening when your parents ask you
to turn them off . . .
at least most of the time.

Now and then,
when the games are all put away and so are the toys,
to be Anishinaabe means
gathering around to hear the wisdom of old,
the stories of the original people and their original ways.

You know some tried to stop us from being
Anishinaabe?
But they couldn't do it.

Our people kept telling our stories about our ancestors
and the dogs that we kept.
Including one dog that farted.
We laugh and laugh and laugh
because we love to laugh.

We will never stop being Anishinaabe.

To be Anishinaabe means
once in a while, on a special occasion,
having a chance to dance at a powwow.
It's so much fun!

And it means
when we head out onto the land and into the bush,
deep in our hearts, we know
someone just like us has been here before.

To be Anishinaabe means
being just like everyone else you know,
but also being just like you.

Miigwech!

Words by Brittany Luby
Art by Corrie Hill

Brave One:

You can learn!

There are many different ways to do so.

It is important to know that learning does not always happen in a classroom. You cannot measure understanding by checkmarks or gold stars alone. Your best teachers may or may not be found at school.

Some people find mentors who can pass on their knowledge through stories.

When I was fully grown, Elders from my ancestral community called me home. They asked me to care for manoomin, a plant relation. I knew Mom made delicious casseroles with manoomin and mushrooms. I knew Native Harvest sold manoomin pancake mix. I knew I had a lot to learn! I felt unprepared for this important responsibility. In a word, I was scared.

Elder John Henry then gave me a story. In the old days, Anishinaabeg organized manoomin fields into sections. One section was set aside for children to practice harvesting and seeding. Through story, John showed me that the land can become a classroom. I was no longer a child, but I knew that together, we could create a safe place for me to learn.

Mentors can also teach by guiding you through a task. Elder Danny Strong showed me, step-by-step, how to check whether manoomin is ready to harvest. Manoomin must reach a certain color and size before you can bring it home. Sometimes, I still make mistakes.

Have you ever watched a fawn learn how to run? It is not natural or effortless. There is a learning process that may require repeated attempts.

Sometimes we wobble like fawns to learn. That is okay.

When I hand-harvest manoomin today, Danny reminds me how to test my understanding. An experienced harvester may be able to work by color and size alone, but texture can help learners like me. If a seed snaps dry between your fingers, manoomin is ready to harvest. If you find a milky paste inside, manoomin needs more time to grow.

You can learn! I can too! Never let anyone tell you otherwise.

Learning may take time. It might even feel frustrating some days. But after a wobble, you can reflect and adjust and try again.

"Smart" is not something you are or are not. Learning begins with a promise never to give up on yourself.

B.

Words by Jessica Johns
Art by Jessie Boulard

Advice for Awâsis:

Cut moose meat very thin, rolling it out to cut it in one long piece. Hang it over the smoke to dry.

Watch your aunties first, then copy them. That's the best way to learn.

Scale fish with the edge of a spoon. To filet it, first cut around the head, then from the head to the tail along the spine. You should be able to hear the sound of the knife along the ribs, like a zipper. Then pull out all the guts and scrape as much of the blood away as you can.

Watch your aunties first, then copy them. That's the best way to learn.

Remember, all you need is a sharp knife and to know you're allowed to be bad at things until you're good, eventually. Learning takes time.

Pray to the east, where the sun rises.
Give tobacco with your left hand.
Wake medicine up before you pick it.
Only take what you need.
Your hand is the best measuring tool.

Wild mint is to settle your stomach.

Birchbark is for your kidneys.

Yarrow is soft medicine, blood medicine. When you pick it, take the whole plant and shake the sand off the roots. If you ever get stung by a bee, rub the flowers on your skin.

Rat root is for your lungs. Pick only the brown roots, not the purple. Chew on it if you have a headache or a sore throat.

Don't eat red willow. You can use it to build instead. Soak the sticks before you use them. Water will make them easy to bend.

Dry fresh medicines on cardboard before storing them in paper bags or jars.

Give the medicine away.

Invite everyone. Exclusion isn't an option. Always plan for more people.

In your first sweat, bring a change of clothes and a big towel. Take off your glasses (if you have glasses) and all your jewelry. Make sure you have water to drink between rounds. If it feels too hot, put your towel over your face. Breathe slowly and calmly. Don't talk during songs or prayers.

Watch your aunties and copy what they do. That's the best way to learn.

You don't need to cut moose meat, scale fish, pick medicine, or go to sweat lodge to be an Indian.

Love your friends and your family.

Accept love back.

You were made for this world.

CONTRIBUTORS

ELLA NATHANAEL ALKIEWICZ is Labrador Inuk and a self-taught visual artist. She likes creating colorful pictures. Ella is a dual citizen and a beneficiary of Nunatsiavut Government. She lives with her husband and tabby.

ETHAN BEAR was born in Regina, Saskatchewan, and raised in the Ochapowace Nation. He drew inspiration from his brother Everett Bear and other Indigenous hockey players, including Carey Price and Jordin Tootoo. Bear was chosen by the Edmonton Oilers in the fifth round (No. 124) of the 2015 NHL Draft. After four seasons with the Seattle Thunderbirds of the WHL, he made his NHL debut with the Oilers on March 1, 2018. He has since played for the Hurricanes, the Canucks and the Capitals.

CHRISTI BELCOURT is a Métis visual artist, environmentalist and social justice advocate. She is most well-known for her large painted floral landscapes of Métis beadwork. Her paintings are found within many public and permanent collections across North America. Christi has also organized several national community-based projects of note, including Walking With Our Sisters, the Willisville Mountain Project and the Onaman Collective. She devotes much of her time to supporting Indigenous language revitalization.

CINDY BLACKSTOCK, a member of the Gitxsan First Nation and Executive Director of the First Nations Child & Family Caring Society, was honored to work with First Nations colleagues and children on a successful human rights challenge to Canada's inequitable provision of child and family services and failure to implement Jordan's Principle. This hard-fought litigation has resulted in hundreds of thousands of services being provided to First Nations children, youth and families. Cindy was the recipient of the 2023 World's Children's Prize for the Rights of the Child, an award adjudicated by millions of children worldwide and referred to as "The Children's Nobel Prize."

JESSIE BOULARD was born and raised in southern Ontario and continues to live there with her husband, three children and their black cat named Solstice. By day, she is an unschooling stay-at-home mom and by night works as a freelance illustrator and graphic designer. She is currently building a nomadic art studio, Lux Niagara. She works in both physical and digital formats, and her portfolio includes work for Crave, *The Walrus* and *Canadian Geographic*.

DAPHNE BOYER, visual artist and plant scientist of Métis descent, lives and works on unceded ləkʷəŋən territory in Victoria, British Columbia. Boyer creates bold, contemporary art using two photo-based techniques she recently invented: digital beading and digital quillwork. Her art, situated at the intersection of Indigenous knowledge and Western science, showcases her Métis heritage and honors plants and animals as kin.

WARREN CARIOU is a Red River Métis writer, photographer and professor based in Winnipeg, Manitoba. He has published works of memoir, fiction and poetry and has devoted much of his career to celebrating Indigenous oral storytelling.

AILAH CARPENTER is a 2Spirited, multidisciplinary artist based in Saskatoon, Saskatchewan. Inspired by adversity, they use art to communicate the "in-between" experience of 2Spirituality, mixed Settler-Indigenous identity, and invisible disability. While pursuing their BFA at the University of Saskatchewan, they actively support community projects and showcase their work. Ailah dreams of one day illustrating and publishing their writing.

CONTRIBUTORS

CHIEF LADY BIRD is a Chippewa/Potawatomi artist from Rama First Nation. She holds a BFA in Drawing and Painting with a minor in Indigenous Visual Culture from OCAD University, and is currently living on her reserve, where she paints and raises a blended family. Throughout her career, she has utilized her personal understandings of Anishinaabek Law and Cosmologies to envision abundance, love and Indigenous futurisms. Chief Lady Bird is known for her murals, children's book illustrations and digital work (which includes an emoji for Twitter and a logo for Xbox, among many other exciting projects!).

CHERIE DIMALINE is a member of the Georgian Bay Métis Community in Ontario. Her 2017 book, *The Marrow Thieves*, was named one of the "Best YA Books of All Time" by *TIME*, won the Governor General's Literary Award and the prestigious Kirkus Prize for Young Readers' Literature, and was the fan favorite for CBC's 2018 Canada Reads.

LEAH MARIE DORION is a Métis writer and artist currently living near Prince Albert, Saskatchewan. Her artwork celebrates the strength and resilience of Indigenous women and families. Leah is also a published children's book author and illustrator. Several of her Métis cultural books are available through Gabriel Dumont Institute Press in Saskatoon, Saskatchewan, and Strong Nations Publishing in Nanaimo, British Columbia.

NORMA DUNNING is a Padlei Inuk writer, professor and grandmother. She has published five books to date, all of which have been translated into several languages. She lives and works in Regina, Saskatchewan.

JENNIFER GRENZ is an Nlaka'pamux woman of mixed ancestry currently living on the lands of the Pentlatch-speaking people. She is an ecologist working to help Indigenous communities heal their lands and revitalize their food systems.

KARLENE HARVEY (she/they) is Tŝilhqot'in and Syilx and lives on the coast in East Vancouver, British Columbia. Karlene has illustrated several children's picture books and is currently working on a comic series. They love stories that explore elements of magic, multi-dimensions and humor.

DEIDRE HAVRELOCK is a Cree, Canadian author. She grew up in Edmonton, Alberta, with a ghost in her house, a feminist for a grandma and wishing she had a buffalo for a pet! She currently resides in Saskatoon, Saskatchewan — Treaty 6 Territory and Homeland of the Métis.

CORRIE HILL is an artist and member of the Kanien'kehá:ka (Mohawk) Nation, Bear Clan, from Six Nations of the Grand River. Corrie has always viewed art as medicine that strengthens her mental wellness and to showcase her pride as an Onkwehon:we.

ALANAH ASTEHTSI̲ʼ OTSISTÓHKWAʔ (MORNINGSTAR) JEWELL (she/her) is a French–First Nations artist. She is Bear Clan from Oneida Nation of the Thames, grew up off-reserve and currently lives in Kitchener, Ontario. Alanah is an illustrator, painter and muralist, and organizes local Indigenous art markets through @IAmKitchener on Instagram. Her passion is promoting Indigenous art and culture in urban areas.

KAYA JOAN is a multidisciplinary mixed Vincentian, Kanien'kehá:ka and Jamaican settler artist born and raised in T'karonto and currently based in Prince Edward County, Ontario. Kaya's practice explores their relationship to place, storytelling, Black and Indigenous futurity and creation stories.

CONTRIBUTORS

JESSICA JOHNS is a queer nehiyaw auntie with English-Irish ancestry and a member of Sucker Creek First Nation. Her debut novel, *Bad Cree*, was shortlisted for the Amazon Canada First Novel Award. She lives in Edmonton, Alberta, with her brilliant girlfriend and their two cats, Alfredo and Olive.

WAB KINEW is an Anishinaabe author from the Ojibways of Onigaming First Nation. He lives in Winnipeg, Manitoba, with his family.

GEORGE LITTLECHILD, born in Edmonton, Alberta, is the son of a Plains Cree mother and a Canadian Celtic father. George was taken from his home as part of the Sixties Scoop and was raised by foster parents. He received a diploma in art and design from Red Deer College and a BFA from the NSCAD, Halifax, Nova Scotia. He also received an Honorary Doctorate from the University of the Fraser Valley. His mixed-media art is often made in response to political movements and societal concerns such as reconciliation and reclamation, as well as personal history.

BRITTANY LUBY, of Anishinaabe and mixed European descent, was raised on Treaty 3 Lands in what is now known as northwestern Ontario. She has been trained by Elders at her ancestral community, Niisaachewan Anishinaabe Nation, to raise awareness of Crown-Anishinaabe relations in what is currently known as Canada. She works as an author and a professor to help fulfill that responsibility.

MAYA McKIBBIN is a Two-Spirited multidisciplinary animator, illustrator and comic artist currently living on the unceded traditional territories of the xʷməθkʷəy̓əm, Sḵwx̱wú7mesh, and səlilwətaɬ Nations. They are Irish and Ojibwe with roots in the White Earth Nation in Minnesota. Maya's art explores the magic of the natural world, both human and not, and centers around the supernatural, grief, nostalgia and curiosity.

PAMELA PALMATER is a Mi'kmaw lawyer, professor and award-winning podcaster from Eel River Bar First Nation. She is the owner of Warrior Life Studios, dedicated to bringing Indigenous stories to life.

DENESEE PAUL is a Dene Canadian artist. He currently resides in Toronto, Ontario, where he works and lives with his daughter Eden. Denesee discovered at an early age that painting and drawing are things that he enthusiastically loves and has been creating art ever since.

MANGESHIG PAWIS-STECKLEY is a multidisciplinary Anishinaabe artist from Barrie, Ontario, and a member of Wasauksing First Nation. He currently resides in the unceded territories of the Musqueam, Squamish and Tsleil-Waututh people (Vancouver, British Columbia). He is an award-winning children's book illustrator whose work explores themes of language revitalization, ancestral-knowledge sharing and memory.

AUTUMN PELTIER (RED MOON WOMAN) was born in Wikwemikong First Nation and currently resides in Ottawa, Ontario. She is internationally known for her Indigenous rights and water activism. She addressed the United Nations at the age of thirteen, was a finalist for the International Children's Peace Prize, received the Sovereign's Medal for Volunteers from the Governor General of Canada and has a cat named Masska. She studies political law and criminology at the University of Ottawa.

CONTRIBUTORS

DAVID A. ROBERTSON is a two-time winner of the Governor General's Literary Award and has won the TD Canadian Children's Literature Award, as well as the Writers' Union of Canada's Freedom to Read Award. He has received several other accolades for his work as a writer for children and adults, podcaster, public speaker and social advocate. In 2023, he was honored with a Doctor of Letters by the University of Manitoba for outstanding contributions to the arts and distinguished achievements. He is a member of Norway House Cree Nation and lives in Winnipeg, Manitoba.

JASON SIKOAK, of Inuit descent, was born in Labrador, and then spent the beginning of their life living and exploring their home community of Rigolet, Nunatsiavut. Since their early days, Jason has traveled the world outside of their hometown and always explored their creative side, which led them to be living in Montréal, Quebec, where they obtained their BFA degree, with distinction, from Concordia University. Jason's practice varies, so they best describe themselves as a "Maker of Things."

MAZINA GIIZHIK-IBAN (MURRAY SINCLAIR) was the first Indigenous judge appointed in Manitoba and Canada's second Indigenous judge. He served as Chief Commissioner of the Truth and Reconciliation Commission (TRC), participating in hundreds of hearings across Canada, which culminated in the TRC's report in 2015. Appointed to the Senate in 2016, Sinclair retired in 2021 but remained active within his legal profession and his community until he passed away in Winnipeg, Manitoba, in 2024.

SARA SINCLAIR is an oral historian of Nehiyaw-Anishinaabe, German-Jewish and British descent. Sara teaches in the Oral History Master of Arts Program at Columbia University. She is the editor of *How We Go Home: Voices from Indigenous North America* (Voice of Witness/Haymarket Books, 2020).

STEPHANIE SINCLAIR is Publisher of McClelland & Stewart. She is of Nehiyaw-Anishinaabe, German-Jewish and British descent. She is a fierce advocate and activist, serving as a mentor, curator and organizer of publishing events to challenge colonial practices in publishing and to advance the work of reconciliation. She lives in Hamilton, Ontario, with her two tiny humans.

BRYCE MANY FINGERS / SINGER is a Niitsítapi mixed-media artist and member of the Blood Tribe (Kainai Nation) currently residing in Lethbridge, Alberta. His graphic-style work explores themes centered around land, history, health, issues impacting Indigenous Peoples and personal narratives on cultural identity. He is a student at the University of Lethbridge, where he is studying psychology and art.

MONIQUE GRAY SMITH is trained as a psychiatric nurse, and her first published novel, *Tilly: A Story of Hope and Resilience*, won the 2014 Burt Award for First Nations, Métis and Inuit Literature. Since then, Monique has published nine books for a broad spectrum of ages that cover a range of topics and emotions. Woven into all of Monique's writing, speaking engagements and online courses is the teaching that Love Is Medicine.

CYNTHIA LEITICH SMITH is an award-winning author of books for young readers, a NSK Neustadt laureate and a citizen of Muscogee Nation. She grew up in Kansas City, makes her home in sunny Austin, Texas, and lives with Chihuahuas named Gnocchi and Orzo.

CONTRIBUTORS

TASHA SPILLETT is a celebrated author, educator, scholar and public speaker who draws her strength from her Indigenous (Cree) and Trinidadian bloodlines. She makes her home in Treaty 1 Territory, Manitoba.

LUKE SWINSON is a visual artist with Anishinaabe roots from Kitchener, Ontario. A member of the Mississaugas of Scugog Island First Nation, Luke's work reflects his desire to better understand and reclaim his Indigenous culture. He seeks to promote cultural education and preservation through his art projects.

ALAN SYLIBOY grew up believing that Native art was generic. "As a youth, I found painting difficult and painful, because I was unsure of my identity." But his confidence grew in 1972 when he studied privately with Shirley Bear. Syliboy looks to the Indigenous Mi'kmaq petroglyph tradition for inspiration and develops his own artistic vocabulary out of those forms.

TANYA TAGAQ was born in Cambridge Bay, Nunavut. She now lives in Toronto, Ontario. She is a musician/composer as well as an author. She makes great lasagna.

ZOE TODD (Red River Métis) was born in Edmonton, Alberta, and has spent their life imagining fishy worlds across the prairies. They are a writer, scholar and artist working and living in Snaw-naw-as, Snuneymuxw and Qualicum First Nations territories on Vancouver Island, British Columbia.

KATHERENA VERMETTE is a Michif writer from Treaty 1 Territory, Winnipeg, Manitoba. In 2013, her first book, *North End Love Songs* (The Muses' Company), won the Governor General's Literary Award for Poetry. Since then, her work has garnered awards and critical accolades across genres. She holds an MFA from the University of British Columbia and an honorary Doctor of Letters from the University of Manitoba.

JESSE WENTE is Toronto born and raised, and currently resides in Etobicoke, Ontario, with his family. An award-winning author and speaker, Jesse is a member of the Serpent River First Nation.

MICHAEL NICOLL YAHGULANAAS is an author, visual artist and mischief-maker. His art lives in many places, including the British Museum, Metropolitan Museum of Art, Humboldt Forum and Vancouver Art Gallery. Brimming with curiosity and ideas, he carries a traveler's ticket in one hand and a sketchbook in the other.

NOTE ABOUT THE COVER ART

The cover illustration draws inspiration from the story "Flight of the Hummingbird." In this story, a hummingbird sees her home, the forest, engulfed in flames. She responds by carrying water to the flames, one drop at a time. When the other animals ask her why she does this, she simply replies, "I'm doing what I can."

I first read the version of this story told by Michael Nicoll Yahgulanaas when I moved out West, during a time when I hadn't yet built a community or found my direction. I had a deeply embedded belief of "never being good enough," and this story resonated deeply within me.

There's only so much any one of us can do to ease the harm humanity faces and make the world a better place. Some can do more, while others may struggle. We all have our challenges and personal healing to work through. It's simply not possible to answer every call to action, and shaming those who can't only hurts our collective well-being. Sometimes, the ones who have the most potential to help are going through their own struggles and need someone to offer them a hand first.

When I consider my own contributions, I think about my skills and limitations. We each have unique gifts — some of us are orators, artists or healers. Others are musicians, teachers or parents. Some are land defenders, standing on the front lines, while some are writers, influencing generations from their desks. We can't do it all; we must focus on our strengths. As individuals, we may be small, but together, we are powerful. And it all begins with a single drop of water.

— Mangeshig Pawis-Steckley

CREDITS

24: Painting © 2024 by George Littlechild
25–27: Text © 2025 by katherena vermette

28: Art © 2025 by Jason Sikoak
29: Text © 2025 by Tanya Tagaq

30: Art © 2025 by Luke Swinson
31: Text © 2025 by Autumn Peltier

32: Art © 2025 by Chief Lady Bird
33–35: Text © 2025 by Jennifer Grenz

36: Art © 2025 by Ailah Carpenter
37–38: Text © 2025 by Zoe Todd

42: Art © 2024 by Leah Marie Dorion
43–45: Text © 2025 by Warren Cariou

46: Art © 2025 by Alanah Astehtsi' Otsistóhkwaʔ (Morningstar) Jewell
47–49: Text © 2025 by Cherie Dimaline

50: Art © 2025 by Denesee Paul
51–53: Text © 2025 by Deidre Havrelock

56: Art © 2025 by Karlene Harvey
57–58: Text © 2025 by Cindy Blackstock

60: Art © 2025 by Bryce Many Fingers / Singer
61–63: Text © 2025 by David A. Robertson

64: Painting © 2024 by Alan Syliboy
65–67: Text © 2025 by Pamela Palmater

68: Art © 2025 by Kaya Joan
69–71: Text © 2025 by Tasha Spillett

72: Painting © 2024 by Michael Nicoll Yahgulanaas
73–74: Text © 2025 by Cynthia Leitich Smith

78: Art © 2024 by Daphne Boyer
79–81: Text © 2025 by Monique Gray Smith

82: Painting © 2025 by Christi Belcourt
83–85: Text © 2025 by Jesse Wente

86: Art © 2025 by Maya McKibbin
87–89: Text © 2025 by Ethan Bear

90: Art © 2025 by Ella Nathanael Alkiewicz
91–92: Text © 2025 by Norma Dunning

96: Art © 2025 by Mangeshig Pawis-Steckley
97–99: Text © 2025 by Wab Kinew

100: Art © 2025 by Corrie Hill
101–103: Text © 2025 by Brittany Luby

104: Art © 2025 by Jessie Boulard
105–107: Text © 2025 by Jessica Johns

Compilation copyright © 2025 by Stephanie and Sara Sinclair
Foreword copyright © 2025 by Mazina Giizhik-iban (Murray Sinclair)
Cover art and interior spot art © 2025 by Mangeshig Pawis-Steckley
except where noted on overleaf.
Individual contributor text and art on overleaf.

Tundra Books, an imprint of Tundra Book Group,
a division of Penguin Random House of Canada Limited,
320 Front Street West, Suite 1400
Toronto, Ontario, M5V 3B6, Canada
penguinrandomhouse.ca

Published simultaneously in the United States of America
by Tundra Books of Northern New York, an imprint of Tundra Book Group,
a division of Penguin Random House of Canada Limited

All rights reserved. The use of any part of this publication reproduced, transmitted in any form or by any means, electronic, mechanical, photocopying, recording, or otherwise, or stored in a retrieval system, without the prior written consent of the publisher — or, in case of photocopying or other reprographic copying, a license from the Canadian Copyright Licensing Agency — is an infringement of the copyright law.

Please note that no part of this book may be used or reproduced in any manner for the purpose of training artificial intelligence technologies or systems.

The authorized representative in the EU for product safety and compliance is Penguin Random House Ireland, Morrison Chambers, 32 Nassau Street, Dublin D02 YH68, Ireland, https://eu-contact.penguin.ie

Library and Archives Canada Cataloguing in Publication

Title: You were made for this world / edited by Stephanie and Sara Sinclair.
Names: Sinclair, Stephanie (Stephanie L.), editor. | Sinclair, Sara, editor.
Identifiers: Canadiana (print) 20240401131 | Canadiana (ebook) 20240401808 |
ISBN 9781774882566 (hardcover) | ISBN 9781774882573 (EPUB)
Subjects: LCSH: Belonging (Social psychology)—Juvenile literature. | CSH: Indigenous letters (English)—21st century.
Classification: LCC HM1035 .Y68 2025 | DDC j302.5—dc23

Library of Congress Control Number: 2024940364

Acquired by Tara Walker
Edited by Stephanie and Sara Sinclair with Kyo Maclear
Designed by Gigi Lau
Production edited by Margot Blankier
The text was set in Goudy Oldstyle Pro.

Printed in China

1 2 3 4 5   29 28 27 26 25